CLUTTER-FREE
HOME
SIMPLE WAYS
to **Organize Your Space**
and **Your Life**

Castle Point Publishing
www.castlepointpub.com

ISBN: 978-0-9981043-5-5

Printed and bound in the United States of America.

10 9 8 7 6 5 4 3 2 1

CLUTTER-FREE
HOME

SIMPLE WAYS
to **Organize Your Space**
and **Your Life**

BRUCE + JEANNE LUBIN

**CASTLE POINT
PUBLISHING**

CONTENTS

✧ OUR SECRETS ✧ ARE NOW YOURS

Even though we've never met, chances are we have one struggle in common: clutter. You don't need to be a collector or live in a tiny home to deal with this issue. Just the stuff of life in a normal space can take over if you're not careful. We've been there! Lucky for you, we've done the hard work of searching for solutions that don't include dropping lots of money at a home store or hiring an organizing professional. In the pages that follow you'll find clutter-control tips that work in your real life.

Each chapter covers one area of the house, so you can tackle the mess room by room as you make your way around your home. With chapter 1, you'll start off in the kitchen and hit the fridge, pantry, and cabinets—even that dreaded under-the-sink space. Ready for the bedrooms and bathrooms? Flip to chapter 2, where you'll find smart ways to overhaul your closet, drawers, and counters. Here, you'll also find clever solutions, especially designed for kids' rooms—including secrets to getting kids to tackle the clutter without complaining. (Raising three boys has given us some experience!) Rework your home office with the advice in chapter 3: Rein in cords, tame paperwork, and organize passwords with a few easy tricks.

Need all-around-the-house cleanup? Check out chapter 4 for help corralling everything from remote controls to holiday decorations. And finally, for the spaces outside your home, turn to chapter 5 to get fantastic ideas to master organization in your garage, yard, and car.

Whichever space you choose to tackle first, you'll be taking steps toward a happier household. **Bring us joy by sharing your victories over clutter with us at WhoKnewTips.com or Facebook.com/WhoKnewTips.**

Together in the cleanup,
Bruce + Jeanne

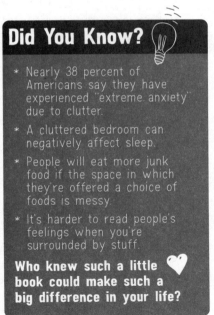

Did You Know?

* Nearly 38 percent of Americans say they have experienced "extreme anxiety" due to clutter.

* A cluttered bedroom can negatively affect sleep.

* People will eat more junk food if the space in which they're offered a choice of foods is messy.

* It's harder to read people's feelings when you're surrounded by stuff.

Who knew such a little book could make such a big difference in your life?

5 DECLUTTERING QUESTIONS FOR EVERY SPACE

How do you decide what to toss and what to keep?
Playing a little game of "5 Questions" can help in any space.

Do I use this? Be honest and answer in the now—not your memories or the someday. Own cross-country skis when you now live in Florida? Chutes and Ladders still on the shelf with no kids or grandkids at the right age to enjoy it? Time to sell or donate and free up space.

Is it extra? Ask any teenager— "extra" isn't a compliment these days. How many can openers do you really need? Can you pare down those shampoo bottles to a favorite? Consider what you really need now and before you bring new items into the house.

Does it make my day better? Even though you don't really *need* an item, it may make you smile or make the day go more smoothly when you use it. It's okay to hold on to *some* splurges, like a few favorite coffee mugs from places you've traveled. Just don't let them take over.

Would I buy it today? This question is perfect for considering decorative items. Does it still match your style or add beauty to your home? Maybe it's time to part with the Big Mouth Billy Bass the kids wanted so badly for Christmas that year.

Can I reduce its footprint? For items you're keeping, look for ways to reduce the space they take up. Can you ditch the original packaging? Combine similar items together in one container? Stash it away out of sight if it's not used every day? Look for creative space-saving opportunities.

CHAPTER 1

FROM KITCHEN CHAOS TO CALM

An organized kitchen saves time and money! If you know exactly what's in your fridge, freezer, and pantry, you'll waste less food. Mealtimes become much faster and easier to navigate when your cookware and utensils are in order. And with some simple kitchen upgrades to make the space less cluttered and more enjoyable, you'll probably find yourself giving in to takeout less often, even boosting your health.

NO MORE CABINET CLUTTER

Easy DIY Drawer

Overcrowded cabinets can be like war zones: You reach to grab something in the back and knock over everything else in your path. That's why we love this easy solution: Turn a baking pan into a "drawer" that you can pull out of your cabinet when you need something. The pan will also catch any spills or leaks, keeping your cabinet cleaner to boot.

Under-the-Sink Magic

If this space is a crowded mess, create a hanger for your spray bottles. Pick up a tension rod at a hardware store, install it inside the cabinet, and hang spray bottles by their handles. Not only will they be easier to grab, but you'll also free up valuable storage space. If your bottles don't fill the rack, add a roll of paper towels for a cleaning station.

Organization on a Roll

Extra trash bags can take up so much space! Big rolls that are cheapest to buy create clutter, even when removed from the boxes. An easy answer: Attach curtain rod brackets inside your under-the-sink cabinets. Then use dowel rods to put your trash bags on a roll. Two rods spaced the appropriate distance apart can hold both kitchen-can size and the larger variety.

Simple Utensil Solution

If your cooking utensils are taking up way too much space in the drawer, consider rigging a hanging system: Pick up a stainless steel cabinet handle and some S-shaped hooks from a hardware store. Install the handle across your backsplash or just beneath your cabinets, then hang spatulas, ladles, and whisks on the hooks. They'll be right at your fingertips!

Handy Hanging Foil and Wrap

Tired of fishing around in a drawer to find your aluminum foil or plastic wrap? For easier access, try hanging them on a wall or cabinet instead: First, get a package of adhesive-backed plastic hooks. Find an unused spot of wall in your kitchen that would be convenient. Stick two hooks turned sideways with the hooks pointing inward to the wall, with enough space between them to fit a box of wrap. Slip the hooks into the sides of the box to hang.

Floating Dry Goods Area

Use that space under your kitchen cabinets for clever storage. Just screw mason jar lids into the underside and create eye-catching, floating mason jars. They make beautiful storage for rice, pasta, snacks, and plenty more.

Free Liner You'll Love

Keep kitchen shelves and drawers neat with window shades. They make strong, wipe-clean liners. Recycle an old shade or ask if your local home center has boxes of scraps and samples.

Custom-Designed Dishware Storage

Do you store glass or ceramic dishware in drawers? To keep
them from clinking together whenever you slide the drawer
open, get (or make) a pegboard with dowels that will fit the
drawer. Arrange the dowels to suit the size and shape of
your dishes or bowls, and they're ready to be stored safely.

Claim Space for Pots and Pans

Don't waste empty space on the side of a kitchen cabinet
or island! Install a towel bar that will keep the pots
and pans you use most hanging with S-shaped hooks
and ready to cook.

Lift Out Lids without Banging

Forget buying one more specialty organizing device when
you likely have a great one already on hand! A dish rack or
V-rack (meant for roasting) makes a great device for sorting
pan lids in the cabinet. You'll end the frustrating time spent
rummaging. Simply reach for the lid you need.

Curtain Rod to the Rescue

Another way to keep those pesky, space-stealing lids in
their place: Mount a curtain rod to the inside of a cabinet.
With the lid's handle resting on the rod, the lids will stash
away so easily on this makeshift ledge! In fact, curtain rods
can create a quick ledge anywhere you
want to lift up storage.

Super Spice Access

Don't have a spice rack? Spices are easier to grab and return when they're stored in a drawer rather than a cabinet. Put small round labels (easily found at any store that sells office supplies) on the tops of the containers, then sort them in alphabetical order. You can add cardboard or simple drawer organizers to keep the spices in line and in the right order. It will be so simple to find what you're looking for and return it to its home again!

Another Answer for Spices

No drawer available for your spices? Divide your cabinet space so it's not wasted and spices don't get lost. Simple tension rods work great to create small ledges for your spice jars.

Packets in Place

Flavor packets—gravy mixes, taco seasonings, and more—tend to get lost in a drawer or pushed to the back of the pantry. Keep them organized in an empty longer-size tissue box. They'll fit perfectly inside! You can cover the box with fabric or decorative paper to make it attractive.

Less-Mess Coffee

Why pay for a clunky, store-bought organizer for your coffee pods (like the kind used for Keurig systems)? You can make your own streamlined version to hide away in a cabinet. All you need is something called T-molding, designed for wood floor transitions. Ask for it wherever wood flooring is sold. To install, simply cut the T-molding to the length of your cabinet. Measure to get the right width apart for your pods, then screw the molding with the flat side facing down into the underside of a cabinet shelf. Your coffee pods will slide between the molding strips in the grooves. Your friends and family will be impressed with your sleek sliding storage system!

Conduct an Annual Review

Do you really need all those spatulas? Keep your favorites and donate the rest. Have food storage containers sitting useless without lids? Send them to the recycle bin. When's the last time you used that panini press? Donation pile. You get the idea, and you'll love the space you can clear for the kitchen items you really need and enjoy.

REVAMP THE PANTRY

Smart Shelf Organization

Make the most of your pantry space by organizing your items by size and frequency of use. Got lots of bulk-size and backup dry goods? Place the lighter items (oats containers, ketchup, mayonnaise, tomato paste) on the topmost shelf, and the heavier ones (giant bags of rice) on the bottom.

Corral Those Food Cans

Canned vegetables can be tricky to store neatly. However, now you can say good-bye to awkward stacks of cans. Grab an unused magazine holder (or pick up a new one), turn it on its back with the opening facing front, and lay the cans inside on their sides—the width of the holder is the perfect size for the length of small cans. Keep them in place by attaching bobby pins or bungie cords at the opening to form a small grate in front.

Paper Goods in Place

Our household seems to collect extra paper plates and napkins from every event we host. But magazine holders can come to the rescue again: Keep the stragglers tucked in them. They'll take up little space and be ready to pull into action on a busy night when dish cleanup would be a hassle!

Downsize on Boxes

If your family is anything like ours, your shelves are always well stocked with cereal. That's why we love this idea so much. We've used it for all sorts of boxed foods—from cereals to soup mixes to drink powders to snack pouches. Downsize the number of bulky boxes in your pantry by pulling out the bagged foods and storing them in an over-the-door shoe organizer. Less cardboard, more space!

Mini Snack Packs to Go

Oversize bags of snacks take up tons of space in cabinets and pantries. To use your space wisely and cut down on overeating, pour the snacks into smaller individual bags—then grab a mini pack on the go for a real snack-size portion.

Elevate Your Snacking

If your pantry has wire shelves, use pant hangers with clips to hang snack bags.

Stadium Seating for Jars and Cans

When you're searching for something in the pantry, it can be a huge pain to shuffle things around until you find what you're looking for at the very back of the shelf. To simplify the hunt for foods in the pantry, pick up tiered shelf risers at a home goods store. The tiered shelving will place items in the back a few inches higher than those in the front. Everything will be easier to spot—no hassle!

Keep Stored China Safe

Stacking fine china? Insert paper plates between the real plates before stacking to prevent scratches. Using storage boxes to stash it up high? Keep your lids in place by wrapping the lidded item with twine—a figure-eight wrapping pattern will crisscross over both pieces and ensure they are secure.

Show Clutter the Door

If your pantry space is hidden behind a door, make sure to take advantage of the door itself as a storage solution. Over-the-door shoe organizers with pockets work well for this spot. Stash anything from spices to cleaning supplies—whatever fits while allowing the door to close easily. Chalkboard-style labels can pretty up the pockets and help everything get returned just where you would like it.

Create Rolling Organizers

Have a space at the bottom of a pantry closet where items just seem to disappear into the abyss? Add castors to the bottom of crates to keep items stored away yet easy to access with a simple reach-and-roll. Perfect for pet food or even potatoes and onions.

5 WAYS TO KEEP PLASTIC BAGS IN PLACE

Sure, you can buy special containers and bags to organize all those leftover plastic bags. But why waste time and money when you have easy solutions right at hand?

Stuff spares into tubes.
Once you've filled a cardboard paper towel tube with bags, stand it in the pantry so it's out of sight. Or tie a few tubes together, if necessary, to keep them all in one place. Stick them in a drawer or stand them up in a cabinet.

Keep them in cans. Coffee cans and chip cans can easily be transformed into plastic bag organizers. All you need to do is stuff them inside and cut an access hole or slit in the lid.

Baby your bags. Baby wipe containers are a great storage solution for so many household items. Both cylinder and box-shaped baby wipe containers work wonders as a plastic bag organizer. Use the linking technique described in the tissue-box tip above to make dispensing so simple.

Tame in a tissue box.
An empty tissue box is great for holding plastic shopping bags that are waiting for their chance at a second life. As you place each bag in the box, make sure its handles are poking up through the hole. Then thread each new bag through the previous bag's handles. That way, when you pull a bag out of the box, the next one will pop right up.

Trash those bags. No, we're not advocating giving up on bags that still have a lot of life! But we do recommend getting smart and storing a few extra bags at the bottom of your small trash cans in bathrooms and other places. When you're ready to take out the trash, you'll be thankful to find new liner bags waiting for you, right where you need them.

FRIDGE AND FREEZER FIXES

Condiments Ready to Go

Bottles getting low? It makes sense to store condiments upside down, but it also makes a mess if caps leak. You can stay organized and clean by storing those upside-down condiment bottles in the bottom half of an empty egg carton. Each cap will easily fit into an egg space.

Smart Bottle Storage

A stack of bottles can save space as you go vertical. Place the bottles on their sides in a pyramid shape, using a binder clip secured on the shelve to prevent a topple.

Hit the Ceiling

You can also make use of your refrigerator's ceiling by hanging metal-capped bottles with a strong magnetic strip.

Level Up with Wire

Those wire shelves that can add a tier in your kitchen cabinets can work just as well in your refrigerator—especially on that top shelf that often leaves too much vertical space to be useful. Think outside the box for clever organizational tools that aren't necessarily designed for a fridge but work wonders!

Simplify Balanced Eating

Organize fridge items into food groups or healthy combinations with baskets. You could create a protein basket filled with cheeses and yogurts. Or gather all your favorite ingredients in a smoothie basket.

Keep Frozen Food within Reach

If you're not careful and organized, your freezer can become a frozen tundra you need to hunt through for bags of veggies. Use magazine holders to create DIY freezer shelves.

Clip the Chaos

Create more room in your freezer by clipping opened bags underneath a slotted shelf with a binder clip.

Sort with Shopping Bags

If you stock up on meats when they're on sale but then forget what you have, you're not alone. Group those dinner options together by type—such as chicken, beef, pork, and fish. Corral each group in a reusable shopping bag to help you organize your freezer. To take it one step further, attach a label on the outside of the bag to let you know the current inventory.

Get Lazy to Get Organized

Lazy Susans work practically everywhere in a kitchen—from fridge to cabinets to countertops.

ORGANIZING LITTLE EXTRAS

No More Disappearing Dish Towels

If you keep a dish towel hanging from the oven or dishwasher handle, you might get annoyed by towel slide as much as I do. Until I found this solution, it seemed like every time I turned around, the towel was on the floor! What to do: Attach Velcro strips or dots in two spots, one on the front and one on the back of the towel as it would hang. Then simply match the Velcro attachments together when you hang the towel.

Cookie Pan Bulletin Board

Kitchens often become Communication Central for families, so it's important to organize those communication channels. We love this crafty idea for a homemade magnetic bulletin board: Repurpose an old cookie pan! Line it with shelf liner or other pretty decorative paper, then stand it against a wall beneath your kitchen cabinets or hang it on the pantry door.

Homemade Message Board

Need a place to write notes for your family? Make a cabinet door scribble-friendly by painting it in either chalkboard or magnetic paint. That way, you and your kids can use chalk to write on the "blackboard" or attach notes with magnets. Alternatively, hang cork tiles for a handy tack-on message board.

Space-Saving Herb Garden

You can enjoy fresh herbs at your fingertips without giving up valuable space on your counter. Try this easy idea: Install a wire shelf between the upper cabinets flanking your kitchen window. Or you can create a plant hanger with just a closet tension rod and some S-shaped hooks. Aside from freeing up space, both of these solutions have the advantages of exposing your plants to good light and at the same time keeping the green babies away from chomping pets.

Hang Tablecloths Like Clothes

Here's how you can prevent wrinkles in your clean tablecloths, ensuring they're crisp and ready to use in a snap. Hang them on a pants hanger! Simply fold one tablecloth over the bottom rung of a hanger, and tuck it into a closet until you need it.

CHAPTER 2

BED & BATH SOLUTIONS

Our bedrooms and bathrooms should be places of peaceful oasis. But instead, they often fill up with clutter and the stress that all the physical mess can bring with it. Sound familiar? You're not alone. That's why we went in search of smart storage solutions and ways to pare down and get organized. Don't wait to bring these spaces back under control so you can enjoy them again!

BEAUTIFUL BEDROOMS

Make Bed-Making Easier

Want to know the quickest way to a perfectly made bed
every time? Stitch a small *x* in the center of your flat sheet
and blankets, then line them up with the center of the
headboard. Presto!

Neat Nightstand Know-How

Streamline your nightstand cleaning routine by keeping the
items on it in a tray. When it's time to swipe the top of the
nightstand, simply lift the tray (and all the stuff on it—a
lamp, alarm clock, vase, etc.), without needing to remove
one thing at a time.

No Room for Nightstands?

Picture ledges can hold more than picture
frames. Use them as inexpensive, wall-
mounted organizers that won't take
away space next to your bed. They're
just the right size to hold your phone and
eyeglasses. You could even add a small
clip-on lamp. Another place picture ledges
work well: above sinks. Pick up some
extras for your bathrooms and kitchen.

Ruffle Up Storage

A bed skirt or dust ruffle can hide more than dust bunnies. Your under-bed space is a great storage area for shoes, offseason clothing, and more. To make an easy, inexpensive bed skirt, run tension rods around the bed frame and drape them with a pretty fabric. Making your own will give you more options and ensure just the right fit. It will also be super simple to remove the fabric for an occasional wash.

Buy More Under-Bed Space

Bed risers are rubber feet you can put under each corner of your bed to lift it a few inches and gain even more space underneath it. Bonus: It feels luxurious to climb into! Look for bed risers at your local home store. Some new models even offer electric outlets and a USB charging station for your phone, laptop, and tablet.

Put It on Wheels

Any old drawer becomes a stellar underbed storage system when you add a simple set of wheels to the bottom. Easy rolling and stashing to clear away clothing clutter or toy overflow in kids' rooms!

Craft Apron Answer

Craft aprons can hold more than your crafting supplies. If you use them along the side of a bed, the pockets can hold books, phones, and stuffed animals in kids' rooms. Such a clever way to organize and keep needed items close at hand!

Stash Sheets Within Reach

Not a lot of linen closet space? Fold your extra sheets neatly and stash them under your mattress. You won't feel a thing, and they'll be within easy reach of where you need them.

Nesting Is Best

Wherever you keep your luggage, stash all your smaller pieces inside the largest suitcase. Take the same approach with extra handbags.

Take the Cake

Tiered cake stands give you space in levels to hold all kinds of small items on a dresser or a bathroom counter. Or you can quickly DIY one using two plates and a candlestick holder.

Organize That Zoo

Stuffed animals strewn on the kids' beds or piled up in the closet? Give them a better home with a DIY zoo cage. All you need is a basic bookcase and some bungee cords to use as the "bars." Simply drill holes in the bookcase to hold the cords. Animals stay contained but easy to pull out when the kids want to play.

Create Magic with Shelves

Floating shelves give you valuable resting spots for books and more while maximizing floor space. The room stays organized and lighter.

Contain the Characters

An over-the-door shoe organizer works perfectly for housing Barbie and friends, action figures, and all their accessories. If any pockets are too large for what you'd like to contain, a bit of stitching can create dividers to downsize each space. You can hang the organizer from the back of a child's bedroom door or tucked away inside a closet. Either way, the toys and your bare feet stay safe, and the room will be less cluttered as the characters enjoy high-rise living!

Stick to Organization

A roll of self-adhesive Velcro can be your best friend when it comes to storing and organizing your kid's toys. Affix the rough, hooked side to a wall in your child's room, and then cut up the soft side and affix to toys. You may even get your child to help you during cleanup time!

Chalk It Up

Whatever type of storage containers you use in kids' rooms, add a special touch: chalkboard paint. Kids love writing or drawing what goes in each container. Now, organizing becomes fun!

ORGANIZED WARDROBE & ACCESSORIES

T-Shirt Roll Call

Maximize drawer space when you put away your T-shirts by using this rolling technique: Fold the shirt lengthwise in thirds, sleeves folded to the back. With the shirt facedown, roll it from the bottom up. Place the rolled shirt into your drawer so the front faces out—this is especially important if the shirt bears a logo or design that will help you spot it in the drawer. Not only will you fit more tees in the drawer, but you'll also find the one you want in no time at all.

DIY Drawer Compartments

PVC pipe is really inexpensive and makes great drawer compartments when cut to size. Just measure the height of each drawer and then cut the pipe to the proper height. It's perfect for storing socks, scarves, underwear, baby bibs and onesies, and little kids' T-shirts.

Get Festive with Socks

Organizers designed to hold Christmas ornaments can work wonders for stashing small clothing items as well.

Bundle Your Panty Hose

Do you paw through your hosiery drawer every morning searching for the pair you need? Cut out the time you spend untangling your hose with this great storing tip: Roll each pair into an individual ball and secure with an elastic hair band. For even easier access, arrange them in the drawer by color, size, or season. Not only will you save time getting dressed and create more space in the drawer, but the panty hose will also be better protected from runs and pulls.

Sock Sorter

To pare down that pile of stand-alone socks looking for their mates, try this tactic. Keep lingerie bags for laundering each family member's socks. It's an easy way to keep them together, and you won't need to sort them later.

Virtual Fashion Organizer

Never spend another morning agonizing over what to wear! The Stylebook app (stylebookapp.com) makes organizing your closet and selecting outfits easier than ever. Take photos of your clothing and label each item by color, style, season, or brand, then mix and match pieces to create new outfits anytime you want a fresh look. You can also add items you've found online to your Stylebook closet—that way, you can see how they'll fit with the rest of your wardrobe before you make a purchase. And, best of all, Stylebook's calendar allows you to track the dates you've worn an outfit or particular piece of clothing: You'll cut down on repeats and ensure that your style is sharp every day!

Track Your Outfits

Organizing experts recommend going through your closets and dressers at least once a year and giving away anything that you haven't worn during that time. A simple way to keep track in your closet: Turn the hanger so the handle is facing outward. Whenever you wear an item of clothing, turn it the other way. It will be simple to see what you've actually worn!

Wall-Mounted Jewelry Showcase

No more rifling through a cluttered jewelry box to find the pieces you want! Mount decorative knobs or hooks to the wall, then hang necklaces and bracelets for an easy-to-access jewelry organizer that doubles as wall decor.

Keep That Cork

When you finish a bottle of wine, don't throw away the cork—repurpose it! Cork is a perfect material for storing and toting stud earrings. Cut the cork into thin slices, then poke the earrings through, put the backs back on, and toss them into your toiletry bag when traveling.

Contain Small Jewelry

You know those small magnetic containers with clear lids that usually store spices? They also make fantastic jewelry holders—you'll be able to spot the earrings, chains, and other small pieces through the lids, making accessory selection simple and fast. Mount these on the wall or against a magnetic surface for easy visibility.

Scrunchie Storage

Are your hair ties all clumped together in a messy ball of elastic and cloth? For an easy-to-access scrunchie and elastic-band holder, use a cardboard paper towel tube! Slide each band over the tube and spread them out so you can clearly see what you have to choose from.

Take Heels to New Heights

Is a shoe collection taking over the closet floor and tripping you up? Use a few tension rods to get high heels off the floor and display them in a fun, organized fashion.

Space for Even More Shoes

If you store shoes on a shelf, here's a simple way to maximize your space. Place the left shoe with the toe facing into your closet, and the right shoe with the toe facing out. They'll fit together more snugly, and you may be able to squeeze in more shoes!

Make Your Closet Fruitful

Hanging fruit baskets are useful way beyond the kitchen. Use them in your closet to contain hats, belts, scarves, or other accessories.

The Perfect Tie Holder

Don't throw away the little Z-shaped hooks that come with dress socks—use them as tie holders! Slip them onto a hanger and they are perfect for hanging the tie that accompanies that particular suit.

Create a Lost & Found

Repurpose an old ice cube tray as an organizational tool for your laundry room. It's perfect for keeping buttons that have fallen off your clothes and other small items you may find in your pockets.

Bag Headquarters

To hold the purse or briefcase you use the most, attach an adhesive-backed hook (such as the Command brand) to the side of a dresser. Your bag will be ready to go when you are and not buried in a closet or littering the floor!

CLUTTER-FREE BATHROOMS

Streamlined Shower Solution

Is your shower loaded with loofahs, sponges, and bath toys? Keep them all in one convenient place by installing a tension rod in the back of the shower and hanging them on S-shaped hooks. You can also use the rod to hang-dry bathing suits, wet towels, and clothing, or as hanging storage space for cleaning supplies.

Save Space with Wall-Mounted Cans

We love this handy solution for storing brushes, combs, and other hair products: Repurpose tin cans as wall-mounted holders! If you like, cover the cans with decorative paper to match your bathroom's design—simply cut the paper to size and glue it around the cans with white craft glue or Mod Podge. Then use adhesive strips (such as the Command brand) to attach the brush holders to the wall or to the inside of a cabinet door. Larger tin cans can even house rolled-up towels. Attach the can bottoms to a painted MDF board for hanging support.

Repurpose Wine Racks

If you're short on space in the linen closet, use an old wine rack to hold towels instead. Rolled up, they'll fit perfectly into the bottle-size slots intended for wine.

Redesign an Old Drawer

A drawer from an old dresser gets new life when you hang it by its bottom as a wall-mounted storage space. Knobs become hooks for hanging storage on the side.

Better with Baskets

Take a new look at wicker baskets and all the organizing opportunities they bring! A square or rectangular basket mounted on the wall gives you instant towel storage. All you need are a few strategically placed screws. Small crates work well as DIY storage units too.

Show Storage the Door

Quick, look up! An easy place to create space: above doors. Installing a storage shelf in this wasted space is smart. In bathrooms, it's a good place to stash extra towels.

Spice Up Bathroom Storage

Turn a wall-mounted spice rack into a bathroom caddy! Use it to store small shampoo and conditioner bottles, soaps, lotions, nail polishes, makeup, cotton balls—and any other items that collect around your bathroom sink.

Hit the Bar

Shampoo and conditioner now come in bar form, just like your soap. In small tin containers, they take up less room and look more sophisticated than traditional plastic bottles.

Clear More Counter Space

Forget that ugly cup sitting out to hold your toothbrush! You can fashion super-easy hanging toothbrush holders from inexpensive PVC piping and end caps. Cut the pipe to the length you want for your holder, add the end cap on the bottom, and drill a hole in the back of the pipe (use the side where there is writing). Install Command hooks on the inside of your bathroom cabinet door, then hang the brushes. You can even decorate the holders with stickers or decals, if you like.

Hairstyling Holder

While you're picking up PVC piping, consider another clever use for it: a holder for your hair dryer and straightener or curling iron! Get the piping section with a joint branching off (called a "reducing Y") so that you have two compartments, and then just paint the thing to make it look pretty.

File That Dryer

Really want to tuck those hair appliances out of sight? Hang a metal mesh file box from the side of your vanity. Adhesive-backed hooks (such as the Command brand) make hanging simple. The metal boxes look great and are nonflammable to hold heated appliances as soon as you're finished using them.

Twist and Blow Dry

Blow-dryer cords can be kept neat using ponytail holders. This will work for any small electrical gadgets, of course.

Tray Together

If your stash of makeup and other beauty products is a disorganized mess, get everything in order with a cutlery tray. Blushes, eye shadows, and nail polishes will fit in smaller compartments, while eyeliners, mascaras, and long brushes can be stored in the larger rows.

Create Sophisticated Containers

You can make storage containers with a high-end look by simply gluing rope or twine around old coffee cans. You may already have the cans on hand!

Downsize Your Travel-Size Collection

We travel a lot and find that mini toiletries tend to sneak their way into our house, only to pile up as clutter. Too many souvenirs from the hotel bathroom or purchased duplicates that you don't need? Clear some space by donating any unopened items to a local homeless shelter, domestic violence shelter, food pantry, or a Ronald McDonald House.

CHAPTER 3

YOUR ORGANIZED HOME OFFICE

Say you need to find an important document or even just a stamp quickly. Could you do it in the current state of your office space? Pens, sticky notes, paper clips . . . a confusion of supplies may be in cahoots to steal your organization and your sanity. The good news: Simple tools, many free and already within your home, can help you get on a more efficient track!

DECLUTTER YOUR DESK

Contain Those Cords

If your electrical cords are in a tangled nest on the floor, get them in order and out of the way: Mount a small basket to the underside of the desk, fold the cords into small bundles, and store them inside. No more unsightly knotted cords!

Can the Chaos

Eat healthy, then take control of office supplies! Just clean your tuna cans after enjoying that sandwich or salad and put them to work corralling paper clips, binder clips, sticky notepads, and more. They'll fit nicely in a drawer if you want to stash everything away. Or jazz up the cans by painting them or covering them with fabric or decorative paper, then leave them on display.

Build a Brick Organizer

Here's a fun idea to help kids get their desks organized or to add a touch of whimsy and organization to the desk of a kid at heart. Simply gather some Legos (we all have at least some lying around!) to build colorful housing for pens, pencils, and crayons. You'll smile every time you put your writing instruments back in their place.

Clear Away Supplies

Do you have a collection of old glass jars and other containers? Instead of allowing them to take up space in a cabinet, put them to good use! Store office supplies, such as binder clips, pens and pencils, rubber bands, and erasers, inside the clear containers—they'll be in one designated space and you'll be able to quickly spot what you need through the glass. To add an extra touch, paint the lids and attach handles to the tops. Fun ideas for handles: plastic toy animals or army men, cake toppers, or decorative drawer knobs.

Safe Storage for Arts and Crafts

Clean out that junk drawer and make sure your scissors, craft knives, and paintbrushes stay in tip-top shape for longer. Recycle glass jars to use as protective containers for these tools, which often suffer wear and tear from improper storage. Cut a round piece of felt to fit the inside of a jar, then place it at the very bottom—this will protect the tips of pencils, scissors, and other objects with sharp points.

Home Base for Notepads

An empty tissue box and some fabric are all you need to make a neat little notepad holder. Just cut the box down to the height you'd like, then cover the bottom section of the box with fabric. Scrapbook or contact paper can work too.

Get Magnetic

We love this idea for keeping important office supplies organized and easy to access. Hang a sheet of magnetic metal on a wall near your desk, and store small supplies in metal tins with magnetic backs—the round containers normally used for spices are ideal. Place stamps, paper clips, tacks, and any other tiny tools inside, then stick them to the wall-mounted metal sheet.

Bring Baking to the Office

Got a spare muffin or cupcake pan tucked away in a kitchen cabinet? Bring it into the office to use as a handy organizer. Place small items inside each compartment, such as binder clips, paper clips, staples, tacks, stamps, and keys. Who knew organization could be so sweet?

PAPERS IN PLACE

Pegboard Fix

Use a pegboard to store important paperwork, notes, and other loose papers, as well as basic office supplies. Insert elastic bands through the holes in the front, stretch them taut, and tie closed at the back; these will hold your papers in place against the board. Put the pegboard into a frame to hang on the wall, then hang scissors, tape, rulers, and other tools from the pegs.

Create a Financial "Hub"

The best way to stay on top of your financial documents is to set up one spot for all related paperwork—bills, bank statements, tax files, and other important documents. Use a large desk drawer with hanging file folders, or get a separate cabinet altogether to use for money-related filing. Your financial hub should be conveniently located near your computer, scanner, and shredder.

Tame Those Bills

Need one accessible spot to file your bills? Use a napkin holder! Even better, organize the bills by date so you know which ones should be paid first.

Simple Sorting System

Is that ever-growing pile of mail giving you nightmares? Regain control! As you open each piece of mail, stick it into one of the following designated files or letter boxes: "Follow Up," "Records," or "Review" (i.e., reread). We also keep a small, inconspicuous trash can near our usual mail-opening spot. That way, we can easily toss junk mail into the garbage without setting it on a table or countertop, where it will sit for weeks.

Cook Up a Mail Solution

Got an extra pot-lid rack sitting around? Use it as a mail sorter! Paint it first, if you like, then organize your mail by size from front to back—small items in the front (bills, postcards, letters) and larger ones (magazines and catalogs) in the back.

Cage Your Mail

Do you have an old birdcage lying around? Use it to hold mail! Hang it from the ceiling, or place it on an out-of-the-way spot on a desk or table, then stash mail, stationery, envelopes, a letter opener, pens, and other writerly tools inside.

Screen Out the Paper

In just a few minutes, you can make a huge dent in the amount of paper coming into your home every day. Simply set up online accounts and switch as many bills and statements as you can to their paperless counterparts. Some companies will even reward you for making the change!

Passwords at a Spin

Have little bits of paper floating around everywhere with usernames and passwords jotted down? In these modern times, everyone is registered for more websites than they can count, making it next to impossible to remember the access codes. Instead of forgetting these all the time, just use an old Rolodex to collect all your logins and passwords right at your fingertips.

TAME SCREEN CLUTTER

Clean Up Electronic Inboxes

Don't max out your email inbox! Keep it organized, up-to-date, and working smoothly by sorting old emails into separate file folders. Create a few general folder categories, such as "Action Items," "Pending," "Records," "Kids," "Bills," and "Shopping." Go through your old emails regularly—say, once a month—and sort them into the proper categories.

Go Deeper Than "My Documents"

Just like your metal filing cabinet has dividers for folders, your computer can be arranged similarly, with subfolders to hold documents of popular subjects. Here's a clever little organizing trick: You can start file names with "aa" or "zz" to push them to the top or bottom of priority space.

Set Up Easy Access

Have a file you use at least a few times a week—maybe a to-do list or a budget spreadsheet? That's a file worth leaving on your desktop for easy access instead of buried in a folder. But limit yourself to just three priority documents of this kind, or your computer desktop will become a sea of documents.

File Those Photos

Digital photos can quickly take over your computer, but they're so much better organized and secure when stored on an external hard drive or cloud-storage system, like Google Photos, Dropbox, or Flickr. Compare the features and free storage space available. You may want to choose a cloud-storage service that syncs across devices, so you can access photos you take on your smartphone directly from your computer and vice versa. Your photos will always be at your fingertips—but not scattered on your physical or computer desktop!

4 SOURCES OF PAPER CLUTTER TO RELEASE

Much of the paper we hang on to is either sentimental or something we forgot about. But if you want to tame the paper tiger, you need to be ferocious in your decluttering approach.

Recycle those instruction manuals. How many of the booklets you've saved have you ever actually returned to? Be honest. If you do want to refer back, you'll find everything you need online. Most manuals can be found right on the manufacturers' websites.

Surrender old class notes. Materials from continuing education—or worse, primary education—need to go. Online searches and the good old library have you covered should you need to look up the information again. If you really can't part with all the notebooks and worksheets quite yet, take a baby step: Scan them to store digitally.

Modernize the inspiration folder. All those recipes, workout plans, crafty projects, and gift ideas you've torn out of magazines…digitize them. Scan them, then sort them onto a Pinterest board (at pinterest.com).

Pare back stationery. How much fancy paper and notepads can one person seriously use? Decide what you can part with and then donate it to a local school or library—where the supplies will be used, not just stored.

CHAPTER 4

FREEDOM ALL OVER THE HOUSE

Shared areas can easily become overrun with the stuff of daily living, from coats and shoes at the door to toys and games on the loose everywhere! Trying to safely stash away special holiday decorations we treasure is tough too. But simple insider tricks can help you regain space in common areas without breaking your budget at pricey container stores.

SMART FAMILY SPACES

Make Your Own Mudroom

Need a designated area where you and your kids can remove
dirty shoes and damp clothing to prevent sullied carpet? Turn
a walk-in closet near the front door into a mudroom! Remove
any items from the closet and install hooks on the walls that
are reachable for small kids (if necessary). Place a large bin,
several boxes, or a shoe rack on the floor, as well as shelves or
containers for gloves and bags. If there's no convenient closet
near the entryway, consider placing an armoire in the area: You
can hang hooks on the doors and use the shelves and drawers
for storage. Salvaged lockers sold on online sale sites can be
great storage options as well.

A New Ring to Organization

Got new curtain rings? Use the old
ones to organize your coat closet or
mud room. Hammer a nail into the
wall, then hang a couple of curtain
rings on it. They can be used to
grasp items like gloves and hats,
or you can run a scarf through one.

Give the Remotes a Home

Where are those remotes again?! You'll increase the chances that they don't get stuffed between the sofa cushions if you set up a centrally located headquarters for them. But you don't need to buy a fancy holder. Just cut away the top of a tall tissue box and cover it with fabric, scrapbook paper, or contact paper.

See It Quickly

And if that remote control still seems to walk away, here's a trick to find it (or anything else you tend to misplace often—scissors, cell phones, keys) faster. Slap a piece of reflective tape on it. The shimmering surface will pop out at you, helping you spot it with less effort.

Cradle Charging Phones

You can clear the counter by creating a mounted phone-charging station. Simply place two small adhesive-backed hooks (such as the Command brand) side by side to hold your phone horizontally near an outlet.

Tame Those Tapes

Stacks of old videotapes or film reels taking up space? You can cut the clutter and make it easier to view all those memories by moving them to a flash drive or DVD or even storing them online in the cloud. This is one decluttering area where it definitely pays to put a pro to work. Check out services like Legacybox (Legacybox.com) or retailers such as Walmart and Costco that also offer digitizing.

Pin Down Clutter

Glue one side of a sturdy clothespin to the inside of cabinet doors, the front of your washing machine, and elsewhere around your home. Hanging clothespins are great for holding plastic shopping bags, and plastic shopping bags are great for holding trash, clean rags, cleaning supplies, and more.

Set Up a Donation Station

Whether it's in your laundry room, mudroom, or hall closet, set aside an area or shared container for items to be donated. When someone is ready to part with an item, they can make a deposit that will be ready to go the next time you make a trip to a thrift store or community drop-off.

Toy Tube Cubbies

Create free storage for toys and recycle empty toilet paper rolls at the same time! Simply glue the tubes together in a pyramid formation to create a little garage for all of those Matchbox cars or a house for all those mini pet figurines. The kids can decorate the storage unit and display it on a desk, dresser, table, or shelf.

It's a Stick-Up!

Have trouble getting the kids to clean up all those toy cars? Magnetic strips are perfect for Matchbox-style models. Attach the strip to the wall in their play space and then watch the cleanup fun as the kids stick up the cars. Look for magnetic knife holders (without the knives, of course!) at home improvement stores.

Buckets of Fun

Who knew plastic buckets could transform into a fun storage unit for little toys? Zip-tie a bunch together in a pyramid shape, building it as high as you need and the kids can reach. This handy idea works well for toy storage inside and outside. And the lightweight buckets can easily be turned to create a tossing game for non-breakable toys as the little ones clean up.

Milk Jug Magic

Don't throw out those empty milk jugs! Cut a large opening in the side of the jug, being careful to leave the handle intact. Then have the kids help you decorate the new creation with paint, markers, even stickers. The result: A lightweight colorful tote for keeping small toys organized. When it's time to clean up, store it on a shelf.

Game Board Storage Art

Game boards can take a beating when kids try to shove them back into boxes that aren't as sturdy as we'd like them to be! Why not store them better and enjoy their colorful art in your family room at the same time? Find or make a display frame to fit each board of your favorite games, then hang them on the wall. Stash all the game pieces in zipper-lock bags taped to the back of the frames so they're hidden away next to the wall.

Create a Kid's Art Book

Are your refrigerator, bulletin board, and various walls around the house covered in one-of-a-kind kid's artwork? When it's time to replace old pieces with new ones, compile them into a keepsake binder for storage, using large plastic sleeves that will hold bulkier textured work like macaroni, beaded, and sparkle art. Leave the binder on display in your living room so guests can view a retrospective of your child's artwork—or store it safely in a box until your little Picasso has more to add.

ADD A LITTLE TENSION
5 SMART USES FOR TENSION RODS

You can pick up a tension rod for just a few bucks at a big-box store. But the ways you can use it to bring organization and a cleaner look all over your home are priceless.

Fashion a stashable drying rack. Even foldable racks can take up a lot of space. Instead, place a series of small tension rods across the basin of a utility sink. Use the rods as drying racks for small items.

Create privacy. A tension rod paired with a curtain can become a room divider. It's a perfect approach to create a temporary guest space, subdivide a room for siblings, or define a private "office" area.

Beautify bookshelves. Want your book collection to look less cluttered? Create little "shades" from tension rods and some fabric to hide messy shelves.

Wake up a plain space. Have a bathroom or kitchen that's not as pulled together as you'd like? Introduce a fun feature that can make the room more attractive: a window awning. All you need is to position two tension rods and hang a stylish fabric over them. Guests' eyes will be drawn to the creative decor and the view out the window.

Conceal that litter box. Kittens are cute, but the accompanying litter box can be an eyesore. Use a tension rod and some spare fabric to hide your cat's litter box in style.

♡ pet

USABLE UTILITY CLOSETS AND JUNK DRAWERS

Handle Candles with Care

Keep your unused candles intact with this easy storage trick: Cover them in tissue paper and slip them into a cardboard paper towel tube. If you like, label the tubes by color, scent, and length so you know what to grab first. No more dented, cracked, and crushed candles in your junk drawer!

Spare Light Bulb Solution

Our collection of spare light bulbs used to be strewn around our closet shelves until we tried this storage trick: We collected all bulbs in their cardboard packaging and placed them in clear plastic bins according to wattage. Lower-wattage bulbs (40 to 75 watts) went into one bin, with the higher-powered ones (100 watts) in another, and specialty bulbs (night-lights, halogen lights) in yet another. Secure the bins' lids closed, label them by content, and tuck them away for storage on a high closet shelf so you can easily see which bins contain which bulbs.

See Through the Junk

Sometimes all it takes is a little inspiration to stay organized once you do an initial clean-out. Line your junk drawer with pretty paper, and make sure you can always see at least a bit of it.

DIY Sewing Kit

We love this ultra-crafty idea for a homemade sewing kit so much, we've passed it on to all our budding seamstress friends. Hit up the farmers' market for a "shabby chic" style of egg carton (a regular one will do too, of course). Then designate the separate compartments for various supplies: spools of thread, buttons, beads, measuring tape, and so forth. Cut a piece of pretty fabric to fit the inside of the carton's lid—this will be your lining. Before gluing the lining in place, reserve half for storing safety pins: Stick a wad of batting underneath that portion of fabric, then hot glue the entire piece to the underside of the lid. Safety pins can be inserted and kept safely in the batting-stuffed cushion. Use the other half of the fabric lining to hold small sewing scissors: Stitch a short strip of elastic into the lining, and slip your scissors behind the elastic. Finally, make a pincushion. Wrap another small bundle of batting inside a new piece of fabric. Pull the fabric taut around the batting, stitch it shut, and place it inside an egg compartment.

Repurpose an Old Candle

You've lost the wick of an old candle, and you were never really crazy about the scent anyway. Turn your old candle into a pincushion by simply sticking pins in the top and the sides. The wax will even help them slide more easily into cloth.

Baby Your Junk Drawer

It's true: Even your junk drawer needs organizing. Make it simple by repurposing baby food jars. Use them to keep screws, rubber bands, thumbtacks, matches, sugar packets, loose change, and anything else that finds its way inside.

Contain That Paint

When you're done with your paint job, save the leftover paint in case you need to do touch-ups later. The perfect container? A clean shampoo, conditioner, or body wash bottle. It will dispense with the clutter of old paint cans, while keeping the paint fresh. If you need to use some, just squeeze it onto a paper plate and get painting!

HOLIDAY ORGANIZATION HELPERS

Protect Tiny Ornament Trimmings

Pill bottles offer a great storage solution for
Christmas tree ornament wires. When you
take down the decorations this year, stick the
small ornament accessories in several bottles
and store them safely until next season.

Christmas Wreath Hibernation

When it's time to de-Christmasize your home, take special
care with your wreath: Place it over the neck of a coat
hanger and cover with a plastic bag from a dry cleaner.
This will protect it from accumulating dust during the offseason. Store the hanging wreath in a roomy closet or in the
basement or attic.

Paper Protectors

We love this trick for keeping rolls of wrapping paper
intact and safe from creases and tears. Cut a slice through
cardboard toilet paper tubes from top to bottom, then slip
them around your wrapping paper roll. For slimmer rolls,
tape the ends of the cardboard and adjust as needed. When
you need some paper, simply remove the cardboard covers
and you're ready to wrap!

A Clean Wrap

Have an old hamper you no longer need? Repurpose it as a place to store gift wrap! Rolls of wrapping paper fit perfectly inside, and you can hang door hooks over the edges for holding rolls of ribbon and gift bags.

Grab It in a Garment Bag

Spare garment bag in your closet? Transform it into a tool for gathering wrapping paper. It's a perfect space to keep gift wrap protected without taking up a lot of extra room. Plus, it's easy to access whenever you need it.

Wind String Lights for Safe Storage

Once you've removed the lights from your tree or around the house, wind each string carefully around a coffee can. Slice a hole in the lid of the can and poke the plug end inside. If you're storing both indoor and outdoor lights, consider labeling each wrapped can with masking tape and a permanent marker.

CHAPTER 5

OUTDOOR & ON-THE-GO IDEAS

Even beyond the walls of your home, you can bring clutter under control! You'll save time, money, and sanity when you can easily locate just what you need in your garage, car, and purse or backpack. Having proper places for backyard playthings can keep them in good shape and away from tripping feet.

GET YOUR GARAGE IN GEAR

Cup Storage

Common plastic cups that you can pick up on the cheap can be great organizational tools. The trick: Mount them on a pegboard. Just drill two holes in each cup and secure using zip ties. An entire board filled with cup storage will keep all sorts of smaller items organized.

Tape at Hand

We turn to transparent tape, painter's tape, electrical tape, and duct tape all the time. But if you're not careful, all those rolls can take over your garage or workshop. Here's a way to keep the tape rolls organized but still easy to access: Use a toilet paper or paper towel holder. Too many tapes to fit? Move up to a full-size tension rod.

Box Makeover

While we're talking tape, duct tape can do wonders to brighten up boring cardboard boxes you have been storing. Use all the fun colors and prints now available to cover that old basic brown box. It's a simple way to make your garage look more like an episode on a home makeover show.

Pull It Together

A magnetic strip is perfect for holding small tools and drill bits within easy, organized reach. Hang it near a tool bench or workstation.

Pipe Dream

Home improvement stores sell organizers for long-handled garden tools at a steep price. But all you need are a few pieces of inexpensive PVC pipe! Cut one "collar" to hold the tool toward the top and one to secure toward the bottom. It's best to cut each pipe on an angle to give yourself clear access to drill and attach these to the wall. You can attach each holder to a piece of plywood or directly to the wall of your garage. Your tools will easily slide into place through the top collar. Label the holders so each tool gets returned to the proper home.

Hang It Up!

Especially in the garage where the fit can be tight, vertical space is your best friend. Walk through your garage and ask, "Can I get that off the floor?" Putting up a few shelves will give you a place to store plastic bins. Even larger items like bikes can hang on the wall to save space.

Look Up Even Higher

The ceiling's the limit for decluttering opportunities! A few plastic bins and a tracking system can transform your garage ceiling into the perfect storage space. You'll find lots of step-by-step DIY systems you can build with a simple online search.

Tidy Up with Tile

It won't add usable space, but sprucing up your garage walls can make it look cleaner and bigger. If you have cement walls, tile is a great, inexpensive choice that will give your garage a whole new appearance. Look for light colors on sale at hardware stores or even your local dollar store. Just apply the tile to the wall like you would to the floor and see the difference it makes!

Take Advantage of Studs

If your garage walls are partially unfinished, look for studs that can help you get organized. Hang heavier items, or add a few boards to the front to make a semi-shelving unit. Bungee cords stretched across can help you contain all kinds of garage clutter.

OUTDOOR ORGANIZATION

Coil Your Cord

Do you have a long extension cord you use with your electric mower, weed trimmer, or power washer? Keep it from getting tangled and running all over your garden's plants with a big bucket. Drill a hole in the bottom of the bucket and run the end of the cord through it. Then coil the rest of the cord inside. The cord will easily pull out and easily coil back up when you're finished.

Help from Hanging Organizers

Sure, they store shoes, crafts, beauty products, accessories, and cleaning supplies inside. But you're an organizing genius when you bring these hanging helpers outside as well! Stuff the pockets with small gardening tools, gloves, plant stakes, twine, and seed packets, then hang it on the wall of your shed, garage, or greenhouse. Hang another organizer near the kids' play area to hold small balls, jump ropes, sandbox toys, and more.

PVC Parking Garage

No more tripping over trikes, scooters, and skateboards!
The kids will be super-excited to park their vehicles in their
very own parking garage. Find a space along a wall of the
house, garage, or shed. Make a simple frame out of PVC
pipe and joints (however big or small you need). Once your
frame is set along the wall, you can use some curved wire
stakes over the pipe to help secure it in the ground. To fully
cover the "garage," cut a drop cloth to size for the sides and
attach it using screws or strong glue. To create an opening
in the fabric, slide some curtain clip rings onto the front PVC
pipe. Then cut the drop cloth to use as curtains for the front
space as well. Finish by attaching polycarbonate panels for
a roof; secure it to the pipe by screwing in a few spots along
the sides and back. The fun and ease of "parking" will keep
the kids putting their playthings away. Plus, covered storage
will protect anything plastic from fading or cracking from
exposure to the sun.

DIY Bike Rack

You can make a simple bike rack from pallets. Just lean
two pallets together, one on the
ground and one against a wall.
Then park your bikes in the
open sections. Pallets are
usually easy to find for
free or at very low cost.

Pool Toys in Place

Noodles strewn across the deck or patio driving you crazy? Pool them together in a smart, streamlined organizer. Placed vertically, a basic wood pallet with a few added hooks on the front can accommodate pool noodles, rafts, kickboards, and squirt guns. Better than a bulky bin!

Buckets Save the Day

Looking for vertical storage possibilities that save space for enjoying your yard? Just screw a couple of hooks into your fence and hang a plastic bucket from each. Kids' outdoor toys stash inside with ease. For a different look, hang baskets—you can find them cheap (sometimes as low as $1) at thrift stores and yard sales.

Bolt Toward Organization

Look for large bolts at any hardware or home improvement store. Then count all the ways you can use them to hang any number of outdoor items—watering cans, hoses, gardening gloves, drying pool towels—to keep them more organized.

FROM KITCHEN TO GARDEN
3 WAYS TO CUT DOWN ON TRASH

You can reduce the trash your family generates and help your garden at the same time with these easy composting ideas.

Bury banana peels. Mix dried banana peels in with the soil next time you plant something new; you'll give it the potassium and phosphorus it needs to grow beautifully.

Turn ash into an asset. Transfer fireplace ashes to your flowers in the spring. Keep ashes away, however, from potatoes, blueberries, rhododendrons, azaleas, and any plants that like acid. And be careful handling the ash: Use gloves and protection for your eyes and make sure you spread it out to prevent clumping and leaching.

Give the garden a coffee boost. Coffee grounds can go straight into the garden as fertilizer to provide nitrogen to roses, azaleas, rhododendrons, sunflowers, and many other plants and trees.

TRAVEL TIPS

No More Disappearing Acts

Use Velcro strips to keep your in-car essentials in place. Anything from paper towels, tissue boxes, maps, toys, and a small garbage can be fastened to a door or seat back. This way, you'll spend much less time digging around under the seats for missing things.

Car Seat Partner

Equip your child's car seat with either a craft apron or a fabric remote control holder designed to hang on the side of the sofa. Either can be positioned under the car seat to hold toys, books, crayons, and all those take-along sources of kid entertainment. And they'll stand a much better chance of staying right where they're needed and not under the front seats, which will make a smoother ride for everyone!

Turn a Cosmetic Bag into a Cleanup Bag

Dollar stores sell these makeup holders very inexpensively. You may even have some lying around your house that you have gotten for free as promotions. They make perfect carriers for all kinds of items in the car! Create a little craft bag for kids on the go. Store essential first-aid supplies in your console or glove box. Stash a bag of nonperishable snacks to keep everyone happy. So many uses!

Loose Change Container

The next time you're heading for a tollbooth, be prepared. Stash any loose change in your car inside a pill bottle, and you'll be organized and ready for paying tolls and feeding meters.

A Box of Bags

An empty tissue box or baby wipe container makes great storage for plastic shopping bags. The box can be easily stored under the seat. You never know when you'll need bags handy for trash, wet clothing, diapers, and more while you are traveling.

Planning a Long Drive?

Plastic clear shower caddies work great to hold everything you may need. Hang them on the back of a seat to be handy for passengers. Or try sticking those little plastic baskets with suction cups to backseat windows to hold crayons or small snacks within easy reach of little riders.

Contain the Trash

A plastic cereal container is a great trash can on the go. It's sturdy and stink-tight, compared to the usual go-to plastic shopping bag. Look for a slim shape that will fit perfectly between the seats in your vehicle.

DIY Travel Size

Be a savvy traveler on your next overnight trip: Instead of buying travel-size toiletries, fill pill bottles with your favorite shampoo, conditioner, styling product, and lotion.

Portable Trash Bags

Hate finding old napkins and gum wrappers in the bottom of your purse? Carry a spare zipper-lock bag or two for on-the-go trash storage. Toss it out regularly, and your purse cleanup will be easier than ever!

Cap the Mess

Have kids you transport to outdoor sports? Always keep a few extra shower caps in your car. When those sneaks or cleats are soaking wet or caked with mud, you can keep the soles from dirtying your floors by slipping a shower cap on the situation.

Portable Art Kit

Moved your DVDs out of cases into a large organizer? Use one of the old cases to hold a small paper tablet (fits into the front cover clip) and a set of colored pencils. For older kids you can trust not to decorate your car windows, include stickers. You've got a kids' art studio on the go!

Cool Organization

Plastic popsicle molds can create small sections in center console spaces. Use them to hold loose change, sunglasses, or extra phone chargers.

Stylish Hanger

How many times has a purse or bag come open to spill its contents all over the car? Tie a pretty scarf onto the handle to hang that bag securely from your car's headrest.

Don't Lose That Umbrella

It's smart to stash an umbrella in your car. But when you go to retrieve it, it's often rolled all the way into the abyss under the car seats. Keep that cover close at hand by securing its strap to your headrest with a carabiner clip. These handy clips work well for purses too.

THE FAMILY CAR KIT

Set up an organized car kit to make your family travels go more smoothly! Chances are, you already have some of these items in your car. Hold them all together in a craft organizing box or storage bin that's ready when you need it. Some ideas of what to include:

* First aid kit
* Sunscreen
* Insect repellent
* Toothpaste
  (works great for stings)
* Baby wipes
* Sanitizing wipes
* Hand sanitizer
* Toilet paper
* Paper towels
* Small plastic bags
  and trash bags
* Plastic tablecloth
* Plasticware
* Individual packs of
  nonperishable snacks
  (such as nuts, raisins, fruit
  bites, cracker packs)
* Water bottles

* Stain remover stick or pen
* Mini sewing kit
* Screwdriver with
  interchangeable bits
* Flashlight
* Deodorant
* Saline solution
* Tissues
* Breath mints
* Lip balm
* Kids' entertainment:
  books, flashcards, travel
  games, craft supplies

DECLUTTERING RESOLUTIONS

I will trash or recycle:

_____

_____

_____

I will donate _____ to _____ :

_____   _____

_____   _____

_____   _____

I will consolidate:

_____

_____

_____

I will better organize:

_____

_____

_____

I don't need any more of these in the house:

_____

_____

_____